D0429613

PAULBALOCHE
THE SAME LOVE
A DEVOTION

David C Cook®
transforming lives together

THE SAME LOVE
Published by David C Cook
4050 Lee Vance View
Colorado Springs, CO 80918 U.S.A.

David C Cook Distribution Canada
55 Woodslee Avenue, Paris, Ontario, Canada N3L 3E5

David C Cook U.K., Kingsway Communications
Eastbourne, East Sussex BN23 6NT, England

The graphic circle C logo is a registered trademark of David C Cook.

The website addresses recommended throughout this book are
offered as a resource to you. These websites are not intended
in any way to be or imply an endorsement on the part of
David C Cook, nor do we vouch for their content.

Unless otherwise noted, all Scripture quotations are paraphrases by
the author. Scipture quotations marked NIV are taken from the Holy
Bible, New International Version®, NIV®. Copyright © 1973, 2011 by
Biblica, Inc.™ Used by permission of Zondervan. All rights reserved
worldwide. www.zondervan.com. Scripture quotations marked KJV
are taken from the King James Version of the Bible. (Public Domain.)
The author has added italics to Scripture quotations for emphasis.

LCCN 2012945041
ISBN 978-1-4347-0526-6
eISBN 978-1-4347-0532-7

The Team: John Blase, Karen Lee-Thorp, Amy
Konyndyk, Nick Lee, Renada Arens, Karen Athen
Cover Design: Thom Hoyman

Printed in the United States of America
First Edition 2012

1 2 3 4 5 6 7 8 9 10

073012

To my Papa:
Roger M. Baloche 1915–2011
You lived well, loved well, and left an
everlasting legacy to your family.

CONTENTS

DEAR READER

In many ways every recording project that I have done is like a journal. Life doesn't stop just because you are in the studio. And life has a way of working itself into the songs and into the process of songwriting. From start to finish, each project I've recorded has taken about nine months. It's like having a baby.

This particular project was a completely different story. *The Same Love* took over a year's time to complete. A lot of things can happen in a year. And in a year marked by personal milestones—my youngest child leaving home, my father's death, my twenty-fifth wedding anniversary, and my twentieth year in ministry—it forced me to reflect on who I am and commit myself afresh to God's calling and purpose for my life.

The songs on this project were meant to help others worship. Often we struggle to find the right words to express our hearts to the Lord, and we find them in contemporary songs, hymns, or ancient psalms.

Psalms are the vocabulary of worship. For years I have practiced singing the Psalms and praying the songs. I model this approach after the Old Testament Levites, who 1 Chronicles 16 describes as ministering unto the Lord through praising God, giving thanks, and offering prayers of petition. Ministering to the Lord in private is the foundation and prerequisite for leading in the public meeting. As we get the words of the Psalms off of the page and into our hearts, we discover all sorts of benefits. The primary benefit being that we are drawn closer to the Lord in our personal walk. We begin to relate to Him relationally—biblically—truthfully.

That spills over into our public role of encouraging worship in the community that we lead in. We start to experience times when entire Scripture verses come rolling off our tongues in the midst of connecting one song to another. It's an exciting realization when you feel like the Holy Spirit is bringing up scriptures that you have stored in your heart and releasing them in a timely moment.

During those private times of singing the Psalms to various melodies and chord progressions alone in the sanctuary, I'm often inspired to capture them with my iPhone's digital recorder, and they become the beginnings of new songs to come—potentially. Either way it's a practice that has helped keep my heart fresh toward the Lord—to keep God from just becoming "my job." It keeps it real for me so that I don't feel like a phony when leading a group in worship.

As I said, the fruit of singing the Word is that I get lots of song ideas. Years ago Ed Kerr and I were invited to write songs for a "Scripture Memory Series." The entire project spanned twenty-six CDs and required a few hundred songs over the course of a year. We would meet at our church office and begin mining the Scriptures, and the Psalms in particular, for hidden gems. We would read them slowly, speak them, and sing them over various chord progressions.

Time and time again we would read a passage from the Psalms and you would never think there could be a song there. But when we would begin singing the Psalms, we suddenly became aware of all these internal rhymes, clusters of alliteration, and other elements that make your mouth want to sing.

An example from *The Same Love* album would be "Oh Our Lord," cowritten with Leslie and David from All Sons & Daughters. The song is derived from Psalm 8. Even if you don't know the melody, sing:

> *Oh-Oh-Oh our Lord,*
> *Oh-Oh-Oh our Lord*
> *How majestic is your name in all the earth.*

As you sing, notice how easily the mouth sings all the "Oh our Lord" lines. They all feel related somehow. Now sing and notice the internal rhymes "How majestIC IS your name IN all the EARTH." Call me crazy, but as I sing the verse with the emphasis on certain syllables, it just falls out of my mouth.

For the past few years I have approached music ministry with the mind-set of a pastor first, and a musician second. We need to be more pastoral in our music ministries, caring more about our congregations getting a biblical, scriptural foundation for their lives than simply singing poetic thoughts. The Word of God is timeless and true, so it's imperative that every generation of believers becomes grounded in the truth of God's written Word.

Our theology or image of God is undeniably formed by the songs that we sing each Sunday. My prayer is that the songs in this collection will inspire communities and individuals to sing these prayers to the God of grace and truth. In this book I unpack some scriptures, share some stories, and offer some prayers.

The Same Love is more than music—it's a life of faith.

THE SAME LOVE

You choose the humble and raise them high
You choose the weak and make them strong
You heal our brokenness inside and give us life

The same love that set the captives free
The same love that opened eyes to see
Is calling us all by name
You are calling us all by name

The same God that spread the heavens wide
The same God that was crucified
Is calling us all by name
You are calling us all by name

You take the faithless one aside
And speak the words "you are mine"

You call the cynic and the proud
Come to me now

You're calling, you're calling
You're calling us to the cross

MARK 5:21–43

As Jesus recrossed to the other side, a crowd was waiting on the shore. One of them was Jairus, a synagogue leader. Jesus was barely out of the boat when Jairus fell at His feet: *Please, please … my, my little girl is about to die. But I believe Your hands can save her.* His words broke Jesus's heart, so He followed Jairus, and the crowd followed Jesus. Of the many pressing around Him, there was one with nothing left to lose: a woman who for twelve years had lost blood plus all her money at the hands of healers whose remedies only made things worse. She snaked her way through the crowd and with a desperate reach brushed just the sleeve of Jesus's robe. She had said to herself, *If I can just reach His sleeve …*

All of a sudden she knew her wound was healed; Jesus sensed something too. He halted the crowd and said, *All right, who brushed against Me?*

The Twelve chuckled. *All these people and You're asking, "Who brushed Me?"*

But Jesus was focused. He looked around. *I'm serious, who brushed against Me?*

The woman knew she was the answer to Jesus's question, so she inched out from the crowd, folded at His feet, and told Him her life's story.

Jesus smiled, ruffled His sleeve, and said, *My brave daughter, your brush with faith has healed you. Go on now, your life is waiting for you.*

Jesus had barely finished speaking when several people ran up. *Jairus, it's too late … she's gone.*

Jesus moved between Jairus and the distraction. *This moment is about you and what you say you believe. This can end here, or we can keep going. What do you say?*

Jairus nodded and they kept on. Peter, James, and John were the only ones allowed to accompany them into Jairus's house. It was splashed with fresh grief, people beside themselves, weeping.

Jesus waded right into it. *Why are you crying? She's only asleep.*

The mourners found Jesus callous and let Him know it. But He didn't care. Jesus drove everyone from the house except Jarius and his wife and the three disciples. They made their way to where a twelve-year-old girl lay motionless.

Jesus knelt and squeezed her hand. *Hi, it's time to get up.*

Just like that the girl rubbed her eyes, stretched, sat up, and started jumping around. Her parents' mourning turned to dancing while the disciples stood speechless. In the midst of the joy Jesus cautioned them, *All of you, not a word about this to anyone. Now, I bet she's hungry.*

A humble father at the end of his rope willing to do whatever might save his little girl. A daughter held captive by the grip of death itself. A broken woman who'd had years of her life stolen by a debilitating sickness. Three very different people with very different needs. Yet each came into direct contact with the very same love, the love of God.

The same God called out to each of them in different ways. Jairus was challenged by "What do you say?" His daughter was roused with "It's time to get up." And the desperate woman heard the strange question, "Who brushed Me?" Each one answered specifically out of their lives, but each responded to the very same love, the love of God.

Shouldn't we admit, though, that even after experiencing this love, we've entertained doubts? And though we have seen answers to prayers, some questions still remain? In this life we experience the discipline of holiness alongside the inevitable humanity of sinfulness. And between these opposing realities, we're daily called to choose to pledge our allegiance to the God who never leaves us, committing afresh to walk the walk of faith. God's unwavering love for us continues, even when ours falters. He's calling us by name, to remind us that He knows our faults and failures. He's reminding us that the cross bears our sin and shame and the offer is to begin anew. And so we walk with feeble legs toward the cross no matter what we have been through, and there He offers us the same love unconditionally.

My mind immediately goes to Peter, a disciple a lot like us. He was faith-filled and trusting one moment, then fighting with the others over who would be the greatest in the next breath. In the course of the same evening he was prepared to defend Jesus in the garden but then later denied ever knowing Jesus, all in an effort to save his own skin. But the amazing thing is that Jesus said on the life and testimony of this imperfect man God would build His church. The same truth holds for us—we are His church! God has opened up our eyes and revealed Himself and taken up residence in our hearts. And He is building His church revelation upon revelation like a builder builds with bricks. The story goes that Peter remained faithful till the end, even dying a martyr's death. After realizing the depths of Christ's love, he lived with a faith he was willing to die for, not deny.

Faith by its very definition is belief in that which is unseen. It's believing that the same love that spread the heavens wide and was crucified and raised Jairus's little girl and sent a woman back into her new life is calling to you today. Your circumstances will be unique to you. Maybe the same love is challenging you to choose what you believe. Maybe you're being asked to bravely step out and let everyone see you and your story. Maybe it's an invitation to get up and get back to the business of living. Then again, maybe that same love is simply calling your name to remind you of your worth in God's eyes. Different times, different stories, different needs, but a love that is the same yesterday, today, and forever calling *Come to me now.*

Take a few moments and look at the specifics of your story. Not someone else's or some caricature of how you think things should be, but the reality of your life. Then ask Jesus, "What are You calling me to?" His standing answer of "love" will be shaped in a way especially designed for you.

Jesus,
there are so many
different voices
competing for my attention,
voices that only know me
as a number or category.
I want to listen only to Your voice
of love, the same one that
calls and knows me
by name.
Amen.

LOVED BY YOU

River flow from your throne
From Your heart through my soul
Healing flood, God of peace
Speak your word and quiet me

I was made to be loved by You
To be loved by You
To be loved by You Jesus

Mercy rain down on me
Hide me now beneath your wings
Hold me close to your side
I am yours, you are mine

Open up wide, your arms and my eyes
Take all I have and make it yours

You've given your life, and now I'm alive
To worship you now forevermore

JOHN 8:2–11

Once again Jesus was in the temple, surrounded by crowds of people. Just as He sat down to teach, a group of Pharisees and keepers of the law stormed in, dragging a woman. They handled her, positioned her in the center of attention, and said, *Teacher, as is obvious, this woman was caught in the very act of adultery. Moses's law demands we stone her. But what would you do?* Their interest in Jesus's opinion was merely a ruse intended to trip him up.

Jesus squatted down and wrote in the dirt with His finger. The woman's accusers pressed in on Him, forcing His hand. He stood up and said, *The first throw must be clean; let an innocent step up.* He squatted down and began writing again.

The older men walked out first. The younger followed reluctantly. Eventually there were only two, just Jesus and the woman. He stood up. *That's interesting. No one left to accuse you?*

No one, the woman whispered.

I don't either, Jesus said. *Go, forget your sin. Remember, you are loved.*

The great A. W. Tozer wrote, "What comes into our minds when we think about God is the most important thing about us."[1] It's a fantastic statement, one that causes us to stop and think about what we truly believe. But what if we take Tozer's words and mix the order up a little? We get another statement, one that's just as mind-blowing. Take a minute and consider this:

What comes into God's mind when He thinks about us is the most important thing about God.

There could be as many responses to this as there are people in a crowded room. But there is only one that is true.

Most of us would refer to the fourth gospel as the gospel according to John. But this gospel does not directly name its writer. Tradition holds that John the son of Zebedee is the author, but his name is never mentioned in the text. What we do have are hints that cause us to lean in the direction of John. One of these hints is a descriptive phrase of the writer found in chapter 13, verse 23. It is almost shocking in its intimacy:

> One of them, the disciple whom Jesus loved,
> was reclining next to him. (NIV)

Imagine a stranger approaching John and asking, "Who are you?" And then imagine John answering without missing a beat, "I'm the one Jesus loves." John believed the most important thing about God is His love for us. That comes out clearly in the first few words of undoubtedly one of the most memorized verses in all of Scripture:

For God so loved the world … (3:16 NIV)

What if a stranger approached you and asked, "Who are you?" Your natural inclination would be to give your name, right? Paul or Lisa or Jenny or Tim. But what would it mean for you to give John's answer: "I'm the one Jesus loves"? Can you see your primary identity as one created to be loved by God? Your identity is really not your job or your body image or the possessions you've accumulated. Our highest value and worth is found in who God says we are, and He says we're the beloved. If you can't see that right now, what's keeping you from not only seeing it but believing it?

This song is a simple prayer built around the truth that God created all things for His pleasure—and that includes you and me.

For in him all things were created: things in heaven and on earth, visible and invisible,

whether thrones or powers or rulers or author-
ities; all things have been created through him
and for him.

—Colossians 1:16 (NIV)

He created us to be loved by Him; it's that simple and
that complex. Our response to such overwhelming good
news is to worship Him, now and forevermore. My hope
is that you might learn to receive His love not only in your
head but also in your heart and soul—in all of you.

It's easy to say that God so loves the world. The more
difficult piece is believing that God so loves *me*.

God of peace,
I so want to believe

26

that You've created me
to be loved by You.
I do, I really do.
Help my unbelief, please.
And even though my belief may
falter, may my worship of
You remain constant.
Amen.

Note

1. A. W. Tozer, *The Knowledge of the Holy* (New York: Harper, 1961), 1.

JUST SAY

I will lay me down here at your feet
Save me from myself and calm the raging seas
You will be my ark that floats me up above the storm

Just say
Just say the word
Just say the word
I'll be made whole

Hear my humble prayer help my unbelief
Speak to me Your hope, Jesus carry me
You will be my ark that floats me up above the storm

Your goodness, your mercy will rescue me
Let your power, your blood wash over me

LUKE 7:1–10

Jesus made His way to Capernaum. A Roman military officer there had a servant who was a good man but was sick, about to slip beneath the surface of life. This officer knew of Jesus and His words, but he wasn't Jewish. He was part of the hated army occupying Jesus's homeland. So he dispatched leaders from the Jews to ask Jesus to come and bring life to the servant.

The leaders did as he requested. *Please, please come with us,* they begged Jesus. *This Roman deserves the best. He is a good man who cares for our people, even going so far as to make sure we have a place to worship.*

Let's go, then, Jesus said.

While they were still a ways off, the officer sent other friends to Jesus, to tell Him: *Master, I'm not worthy of your time and trouble, much less a personal visit. Just say the word and I believe my servant will live. I am a soldier,*

I understand rank and authority, and I trust Yours. Just say the word.

The officer's faith caught Jesus off guard. Turning to the crowd, He said, *This is beautiful! This Roman soldier understands how it works. Most Jews aren't anywhere close to this level of trust, and they should know better.*

When the officer's friends got back to his house, they found it brimming with joy, the servant alive and well.

In the church services I grew up on, there was a time when we were encouraged to take an inventory of our hearts to see if there was anything sinful that would come between God and ourselves, sin that could keep us from approaching God.

Broken fellowship with the Lord keeps us from fully living. We are broken in so many ways, but if we could lay hold of the truth that Jesus has authority to heal the sick, forgive sin, revive relationships, and restore peace in the midst of troubling circumstances, then we would be made whole again. The Bible records these words in 1 John 1:9—"If we confess our sins, he is faithful and just and will forgive us our sins and purify us from all unrighteousness" (NIV).

There are times when we can't find the words to convey what we're feeling. In those times we can simply lift our hearts to God in humility and whisper, "Jesus, have mercy. Just say the word and I will be made whole." Jesus is our anchor in the storm. He is our safe harbor. He is the ark of our salvation.

Lord, I am not worthy of You,
but only say the word.
Say the word, and I will be healed.
Say the word, and I will be made whole.

Say the word, and I can approach You
with boldness
and a clean conscience.
Amen.

CONTRIBUTING VOICES

It didn't feel like we were writing a song, but rather more like a small worship service shared between three new friends. We spent time just sitting and praying for people that we knew in our lives that needed a healing from God. We started to sing the phrase "Just say, just say the word, I'll be made whole." We all felt the presence of God in the room, and the song "Just Say" came out of our hearts as we prayed things like, "You will be my ark, that floats me up above the storm." This song was ordained by God to be heard in moments of struggle, whether physical, mental, or spiritual. If you look to God and believe, He can make you whole again. He can take the most broken life and piece it back together. With just one word from heaven, God really can change a life.

What I remember the most about writing this song is the unity that was present among three new friends. And also

Paul's heart for the people and music directed at God. That's what worship draws you into, community with others of like-mindedness. When three or more gather in His name we can't help but pull out some guitars or sit around a piano and sing our prayers to our God.

—The Brothers McClurg

WE ARE SAVED

Who compares to you
Son of God with open arms
Crucified for us
You gave it all to win our hearts

We stand amazed at the work of the cross
We are saved, we are saved
Our sin has been forgiven
You have broken every chain
We are saved, we are saved

From the grave you rose
Turned our shame into your praise
We stand by grace alone
You have made a way where there was no way

All the honor, forever
Jesus be lifted higher
We owe it all to you

MARK 16:1–8

Sunrise found three women on their way to the tomb—
Mary Magdalene, Mary the mother of James, and Salome.
They were carrying spices to anoint His body, along with
this pressing question: *Who will help us roll away the stone
that covers the tomb?*

As they looked up it was clear someone or something
had already answered their question. The massive stone
had been rolled back, so they walked inside. They were
stunned to see a young man robed in white sitting to the
right.

He spoke to the three: *Don't be afraid. You're looking for yesterday's Jesus, the one they crucified. But He's not here; look, see for yourselves. Today's Jesus is alive, and He's waiting for you in Galilee. Go find Peter and the other disciples and tell them this good news!*

The three women shuddered and fled from the tomb, scared to death but running for their lives.

This resurrection story doesn't involve just one woman, but three. I guess it could have been an individual's witness, but it wasn't. In the divine ordering of the story, God preferred plural to singular, the "we" to the "me." That preference runs so counter to the narcissistic attitude found so often in our culture. We'd like to blame it on the culture or some other scapegoat, but that's an interior struggle we all face, isn't it? I mean think about it, when you see a group picture and you're a part of the group, who do you try and find first? Yeah, me, too; I try and find myself—that's who I want to see.

That's one of the reasons I love collaborative efforts like this album. They are an intentional effort to not only remember but practice the truth that it's not just me, but us.

Jason Ingram and Ben Fielding worked with me on this song. We were trying to press into new ways of saying this phrase we've heard numerous times: *Jesus saves*. As we wrestled with words and phrases, there was this awareness of "us" and "we"—the corporate nature you find, for example, in Ephesians 1:3–12 (NIV):

> Praise be to the God and Father of our Lord Jesus Christ, who has blessed *us* in the heavenly realms with every spiritual blessing in Christ. For he chose *us* in him before the creation of the world to be holy and blameless in his sight. In love he predestined *us* for adoption to sonship through Jesus Christ, in accordance with his pleasure and will—to the praise of his glorious grace, which he has

freely given *us* in the One he loves. In him *we* have redemption through his blood, the forgiveness of sins, in accordance with the riches of God's grace that he lavished on *us*. With all wisdom and understanding, he made known to *us* the mystery of his will according to his good pleasure, which he purposed in Christ, to be put into effect when the times reach their fulfillment—to bring unity to all things in heaven and on earth under Christ.

In him *we* were also chosen, having been predestined according to the plan of him who works out everything in conformity with the purpose of his will, in order that *we*, who were the first to hope in Christ, might be for the praise of his glory.

The struggling continued, and the phrase *Jesus saves* became *we are saved*. This change was not to take anything away from the name of Jesus but to cut down to the very reason He was crucified. Jesus willingly gave His all to forgive *our* sin, to break *our* chains, to save *us*. Yes, I can say with assurance, "I am saved," but the deeper truth, the one that drives me to my knees is that "we are saved."

But here's something. That "we" includes not just the people we like or who agree with us. In other words, it's not just the people on our side. That "we" covers a multitude of sinners; those like us and those quite different, but sinners just the same. So singing "we are saved" is definitely praise to the Son of God, but it is also a challenge to us, His sons and daughters, to realize how deep and how wide is the love of our God.

Son of God,
forgive us for looking in
empty tombs.
You're not there.
Give us courage to run ahead

and meet You in those Galilee places.
May everything we do
be a testimony that
You are God,
and we are saved.
Amen.

ALL BECAUSE OF THE CROSS

What can wash away my sin
Nothing but the blood of Jesus
What can make me whole again
Nothing but the blood of Jesus

For my pardon this I see
Nothing but the blood of Jesus
For my cleansing this my plea
Nothing but the blood of Jesus

All because of the cross
We are white as snow
All because of what you've done
There's a cleansing flow
For all who come
Lord we come

This is all my hope and peace
Nothing but the blood of Jesus
This is all my righteousness
Nothing but the blood of Jesus

Oh the blood of Jesus
Oh the blood of Jesus

On the cross our sin erased

In your death our life was raised

MARK 15:6–20

It was an expected part of Passover to see a prisoner set free. The will of the people customarily decided who that would be. One of the men in prison at the time was called Barabbas. In the uprising against Rome, he got caught up with the rebels and committed murder.

Pilate sensed the crowd itching for a pardon, so he beat them to the question: *Should I release the king of the Jews?*

By this time Pilate could read the hearts of the high priests; he knew expediency was the name of their game. But he hoped the crowd would side with the man they had cheered so loudly just a few days before. Unfortunately, the high priests fueled the crowd to ask for Barabbas instead.

Pilate gave it another try: *So what should I do with the king of the Jews?*

They raised their voices: *Crucify him!*

Pilate immediately countered: *But for what crime?*

The many voices became one: *Crucify him!*

Pilate knew the crowd's desire. Pilate satisfied it. He set Barabbas free. As for Jesus, Pilate had Him whipped and readied to die.

Then Jesus was led from one crowd to another. Soldiers escorted Him into the palace where the entire company of soldiers waited. They put a purple robe on His shoulders and wove a crown of thorns for His head. And then they began their taunts: *Look who we have here, the king of the Jews!* Their words were combined with repeated blows to His head. They spit on Him and dropped to their knees in mockery. When they'd had enough, they stripped Him of the purple robe and returned Him to His clothes. Then they led Him from the palace to be crucified.

It all started with a riff. Ben would play this brooding musical hook repeatedly for about six months until we eventually turned it into this song. The heart comes from the old hymn "Nothing but the Blood," written by Baptist preacher Robert Lowry back in 1876. It's a beautiful hymn the church has faithfully sung for years. I very much wanted to create something similar based on the verse melody of this song, a simple anthem the church would sing for years to come.

Come to think of it, it actually all started with the rift, that fundamental break between God and man. We may not have been there in the garden so long ago, but we've all eaten of that fruit before, we've all fallen short of His glory. As a result there is no one righteous; we've all offended God. And in a very real sense, we all had hell to pay. But because of the cross, because of the blood of the Savior, our status changed from guilty to pardoned.

Pardon. The word can be used as a noun or verb, and the definition deals with the excusing of an offense without exacting a penalty. It's a release from the legal penalties of an offense. Its roots come from an Old French/medieval Latin word for "to forgive freely."

Famous pardons include names like Jimmy Hoffa, Richard Nixon, Patty Hearst, George Steinbrenner … and Barabbas. And then there's the not quite so famous, like you and me.

I don't know very many people who aren't aware of their failures, shortcomings, mistakes, transgressions, whatever we call them. We may not talk about them all the time, as most of us try hard to keep it all looking good on the outside, but most of us are aware, sometimes painfully aware, of our sin. But what about an awareness, maybe even a painful one, of our pardon? On the cross our sin was erased, washed away, and the penalty for our offenses is gone as well. But it was someone and something on the cross that brought about this amazing feat: it was Jesus and His blood. Nothing but the blood could wash away our sin and leave us white like snow. Nothing else, nothing but Jesus and His blood.

Jesus,
give us eyes to see
Who we have here—You.
It's all because of what
You've done—our pardon,
our hope, our peace,
our righteousness.

Nothing but Your cross,
Nothing but Your blood,
Nothing but You, Jesus.
Amen.

YOUR BLOOD RAN DOWN

Your blood ran down
Your blood ran down
Your blood ran down
Your blood ran down

From your head, down your face
From your hands to your feet
Your blood ran down for me

LUKE 23:32–46

Two other criminals were to be crucified that day. When they reached the hill, the soldiers crucified all three. Jesus was in the middle between the other two.

There in the middle of it all, He pleaded, *Father, they don't realize … forgive them, all of them.*

Some rolled dice for His clothes while the rest of the people just stood and stared. A few defiant ones threw ifs: If *He's the savior, He can save himself.* If *He's God's chosen, then He can choose to live.* The soldiers joined in the mockery, offering Him sour wine and still another chance to save Himself. The words written above His head said it all:

This one is the king of the Jews

From His place in the middle, Jesus heard one of the criminals. *You're supposed to be our savior, right? Then do someth—*

The other criminal cut him short. *Have you lost all sense? We're getting what we deserve, but this man's death is senseless.* Then he begged, *Jesus, please don't forget about me.*

Jesus assured him, *I won't. I'll see you soon, in paradise.*

As noontime approached, everything grew dark, a thick blackness covering everything for hours. It was as if the sun could not shine. The temple veil tore right down the middle as Jesus raised His cry: *Father, I am Yours.* Those were the last words of Jesus; they said it all.

I carried this little song around for about five years. It was birthed after I saw the movie *The Passion of the Christ*—Mel Gibson's brutal, uncomfortable portrayal of Christ's final days before the cross. I went back to the piano and this phrase kept spilling over and over: *Your blood ran down … Your blood ran down.* The film left me undone; there was so much blood. I was left crying out of this mix of sadness and gratefulness, reminded of Paul's words:

But God demonstrates his own love for us in this: While we were still sinners, Christ died for us.

—Romans 5:8 (NIV)

It's a very simple song, almost a mantra. Yet there's also a complexity in what is being expressed. For so few lines, it's an incredibly incarnational song. There is the God-in-the-flesh aspect in words like *head*, *face*, *hands*, and *feet*. But there's also this directional word—*down*—that's like a nuanced drumbeat. It reminds us that the incarnation had a direction; it was God's intentional humbling, His coming "down."

Who, being in very nature God,
did not consider equality with God something to be used
to his own advantage;
rather, he made himself nothing
by taking the very nature of a servant,
being made in human likeness.
And being found in appearance as a man,

he humbled himself
by becoming obedient to death—
even death on a cross!

—Philippians 2:6–8 (NIV)

Yes, it was true at the cross, but it has also been true from the very beginning. The blood of Jesus has always been flowing down toward a world so desperately in need. My hope and prayer is that this song stirs up a profound humility and gratitude in people.

If you haven't seen *The Passion of the Christ*, I do recommend it but with a note of caution. Please hear me, it is very hard to watch; there is so much blood. But it does present a picture of what this simple song is all about: the blood of Jesus, running down for you and me.

Forgive us, Lord,
if and when the cross
and Your blood running down
become common.
We know in our heads that
so much blood equates to so much love.
Help us to sense that on our faces,
feel it with our hands, and follow
it with our feet.
So much love ... so much love.
Amen.

SHOUT FOR JOY

Pour out your fervent praise
There's a song to raise
Like a banner high
Lift up your grateful heart
To the Morning Star
He's alive and here with us

Shout for joy
For the Son of God is the Saving One
He's the Saving One
Shout for joy
Look what Love has done
He has come for us
He's the Saving One

We stood on sinking sand
He reached out his hand
Brought us to His side
We turned our hearts away
He was strong to save
Now our Savior reigns in us

Jesus you have saved us
Be glorified

MATTHEW 14:25–33

Just before dawn Jesus started toward them, walking on the water's surface. This sight reduced the grown disciples to terrified children. *Look! It's a ghost!*

But Jesus quickly reassured them. *You must be brave. It's Me.*

That was all Peter needed to hear. He called back, *If it's really You, then tell me to walk to You on the water.*

Jesus said, *Come on then.*

Peter swung his legs over the edge onto the surface of the sea and started walking toward Jesus. But fear, in the form of the wind and waves, crept up his legs. He started sinking.

Save me, Lord! Save me! he cried.

Jesus rushed and caught him. *You started out brave, what happened?*

The wind calmed as soon as they climbed back into the boat. The other disciples witnessed the whole thing and worshipped Jesus, declaring, *There's no doubt about it. You are the Son of God.*

Some songs are vertical; they're sung from us to God. And then some songs are not necessarily vertical; they're songs we sing alongside one another. They're still about God and His glory. One is not better than the other; they're just different types of songs. "Shout for Joy" is not necessarily a vertical song.

Jason helped me with this one. We had been talking about a noticeable absence in many worship songs, not to mention churches: we were missing joy. We both believe that joy should be the sound of the church, the "joyful noise" of which Scripture speaks.

All of us have had moments like Peter had. We get a glimpse of Jesus's glory and it's just enough to bolster our faith. We hear Him speak some version of *Come on then*, so we set out walking on the surface of nonsense. Aren't those first steps wonderful? Absolutely thrilling? But then the people around us, usually those closest like our family and friends, see what we're doing and their voices immediately urge caution and some form of "testing the spirits." The voices in our heads tend to encourage the same discretion, often at a louder volume. When we divert our attention from Jesus, then things start going south. And so we cry out *Save me, Lord! Save me!* And He does.

But how many times, after being rescued, are we dripping with guilt and shame instead of joy? Oh, we're grateful enough to have been saved, but we're really disappointed in ourselves that we didn't get farther on the water. And the absence of joy in our songs and churches and lives is no one's fault but our own. So it's good that we sing horizontally every once in a while so we can remind ourselves of the vertical saving grace of Jesus. His is the only grace that saves. There's no doubt about it, He is the Son of God!

When Jason and I worked on this song we were at his place, walking around the couch with our guitars, singing out loud *Shout for joy! Look what Love has done.* I'd encourage you to sing this one in the company of others. Some will be walking, some will be sinking, some confident, some afraid. But we are all loved by the Saving One, and He is reaching in love.

Saving One,
instead of sinking down in shame
may we raise up banners of
joy to Your holy name.
You have saved us,
we believe that.
You are saving us even now,
we trust that.
You will save us for all eternity,
we hope that.
Amen.

OH OUR LORD

Oh – Oh – Oh our Lord
Oh – Oh – Oh our Lord
How majestic is your name in all the earth

We behold the breaking dawn
The light that shines over everyone
We look to you, we long for you Oh Lord

We behold the rising sun
The earth awakes your hope has come
We look to you, we long for you Oh Lord

We behold the falling rain
Like waters rise flood this place
We reach for you; we cling to you Oh Lord

Oh your name is a light in the darkness
Oh your name is the word of truth
Oh your name, oh your name

ROMANS 8:18–27

It's impossible to compare today's pain with tomorrow's joy. The whole of creation, and that includes us, is being detained. It's not time yet. That's frustrating, but God wants to make sure every piece is in place so that when it is time, the result will be like nothing the world has ever seen.

Everywhere creation is groaning, and this includes us, too. Even though we have God's Spirit within us, there is still the matter of this fallen world and its sufferings. We groan for the time when all will be made new. This is a part of the working out of our salvation, hoping for that which we cannot yet see. So we wait in expectation.

The Holy Spirit is with us in this waiting. Let's face it, there are times when we just don't know how to pray, but the Spirit is right there to interpret our groans, to make sense when little else does. God's Spirit knows things about us that we don't even know, so we can trust in His promise—everything, and I mean everything, is moving in the direction of good.

We can blame it on a number of things, probably too many things to mention, but the result in our lives is that we've grown impatient. We've lost the ability to long for much of anything. And I'm afraid that's a tragic loss. How do we remedy that?

I was thrilled to work on this song with Leslie Jordan and David Leonard of All Sons & Daughters. There is so much to the lyrics, but our hope was that, from the very first lines, this song would be a signal to *behold*, to stop and stand before God and consider the majesty and glory of His creation. To that end, we saw this song very much in the tradition of some of the Psalms, for example Psalm 8 (NIV):

> LORD, our Lord,
>> how majestic is your name in all the earth!
> You have set your glory
>> in the heavens.
> Through the praise of children and infants
>> you have established a stronghold against your enemies,
>> to silence the foe and the avenger.
> When I consider your heavens,
>> the work of your fingers,
> the moon and the stars,
>> which you have set in place,
> what is mankind that you are mindful of them,

human beings that you care for them?
You have made them a little lower than the
angels
and crowned them with glory and honor.
You made them rulers over the works of your
hands;
you put everything under their feet:
all flocks and herds,
and the animals of the wild,
the birds in the sky,
and the fish in the sea,
all that swim the paths of the seas.
Lord, our Lord,
how majestic is your name in all the
earth!

Creation is our ally in recovering this lost sense of longing. I have to tell you there's nothing formulaic about this; you have to literally stop and pay attention to His handiwork. Do you remember the old caution at railroad crossings? Yes: stop, look, and listen. This is exactly the encouragement we hoped to achieve with this song, and we wanted it to be for people all along the spectrum of the church. Our prayer is that the stopping and looking and listening will deepen the ache and heighten the longing for God to make all things new and good again.

I also have to tell you that paying attention to that degree will inevitably cause groaning in our spirits, because for now all is not well. There are wars and rumors of wars and falling economies and rising anxieties and murder and gossip and despair. The recurring temptation in moments like these is to lose our words for prayer, to falter in our trust that all things will one day be well. Praise God that His Spirit is right there taking those groans, those "ohs" of beholding, and turning them into the "ohs" of adoration.

Oh Lord, our Lord,
teach us the art of beholding

the work of Your hands,
the stars in the sky,
the fish in the sea,
and everything in between.
Thank You that even
though our words might
fail us, You never will.
Oh Lord, our Lord,
we reach out to You.
Amen.

CONTRIBUTING VOICES

*Stepping into the writers' room that morning, my palms were
sweating and my heart was working at a quick pace. David
and I were waiting for Paul Baloche to arrive and couldn't be
more excited for the opportunity to meet and write with such
an influential leader and writer. I had looked up to Paul for
a long time, and so it came as no surprise when he showed up
and greeted us with hugs and a smile! We jumped right in to
getting to know one another and talking about our churches.
We had that in common—we had a deep love for the people
in our churches. And we wanted to write songs that we could
sing together.*

*Paul began to pray over our time and asked God's spirit
to come and dwell with us in that moment. And then he
began to sing the word* BEHOLD! *"We behold you God. We
behold your beauty. We behold your majesty and love." As
we looked to the Lord for words, David began reading from
Psalm 8, and this beautiful phrase was spoken and stayed
there, hanging in the room around us: "Oh Lord, our Lord
how majestic is your name in all the earth." It quickly became
the light for the path of this song. It didn't take long for "Oh
Our Lord" to fill our lungs and hearts. We knew it would*

become a song that our churches would sing! Our time with Paul and with that moment of beholding God's glory will stay with us as long as time allows!

—Leslie Jordan, All Sons & Daughters

MY HOPE

Nothing will change if all the plans I make go wrong
Your love stays the same
Your light will guide me through it all
I'm hanging on, I'm leaning in to You

Nothing can reach the end of all Your faithfulness
Your grace is with me
Through every shadow, every test
I'm hanging on, I'm leaning in to You

I don't know where You'll take me
But I know You're always good

My hope is built on nothing less
Than Your great love, Your righteousness
I will not walk another way

I trust Your heart, I trust Your Name
I'm holding on, I'm holding on to You

You are my rock when storms are raging all around
You shelter me God
I'm safe with You on solid ground
I'm hanging on, I'm leaning in to You

I don't know where you'll take me
But I know you're always good

I'm holding on, I'm holding on to You

MARK 5:1–20

Their journey took them to the other side, Gerasene country. Jesus was barely out of the boat when a wild man appeared, one who lived off to the side, out among the dead. Many had tried to geld him, but his strength was beyond them. He spent his time wandering the hills—crazed, bloodied, homesick. As soon as he caught sight of Jesus he started for Him, running and falling at His feet.

The man cried, *Mercy, please Jesus, Son of the Highest God. Please have mercy!* The wild man said this because Jesus kept roaring at the darkness behind his eyes: *Enough! Enough!*

Jesus asked, *How are you known?*

The evil replied, *I am Many, there are many of us. Please, please don't exile us.* The evil noticed a drove of pigs close by and pleaded, *There, drive us into them.*

Jesus granted their request. All the evil rushed from man to beasts. It was more than pigs could handle, so the herd pitched down the hillside into the sea and their end.

The witnesses to this exorcism fled the scene and told everyone they saw what had happened. And everyone dropped what they were doing to go and see for themselves. What they found didn't make sense; the man-once-many was now simply himself. The witnesses gave their accounting, including the loss of two thousand pigs. Jesus was more than the crowd could handle, and they drove Him back to the boat.

Jesus had barely stepped back into the boat when the man-now-free pleaded to come along. Jesus refused his request: *No, go back home and amaze them with your tale of hope.*

And so he did, spreading his story of wonder throughout Decapolis.

This was one of the last songs written for the project. And it was really birthed out of this past year of my life, one of the most uncertain years I've experienced in a long time. There were little things along the way that caught me off guard, but there were three larger pieces that left me feeling a lot like the man who lived among the tombs: my father died, my mother was diagnosed with Alzheimer's disease, and our kids moved away to pursue their lives and dreams. I kept saying, *Please, mercy, enough! Enough!* But it was like the hard things just kept coming; they refused to let up.

Ed Kerr was the principal cowriter on this song. Ed and I spent several years working together in the early days of our church. We would meet early in the morning—read the Word, drink coffee, and write songs, not necessarily in that order. We wrote hundreds of songs back in those days, so it was a joy to reunite with him on this song. Ed had come out for a mutual friend's wedding and stayed with us. What came out of the time with Ed was this hope-filled line: *just hang on to the love of God, don't let go, just hang on.*

The phrase *hang in there* can be a trite expression, sort of like *bless your heart.* It holds little or no concern for the other person's actual situation; it's just something to say, usually to make us feel better about ourselves. But I am a witness that it can also be incredibly powerful, because sometimes there's simply nothing else to hold onto other than the love of God. Sometimes it's all we can do. And those may be just the times when we approach the true meaning of faith—holding on, hanging on.

I have to say a huge thank you to Kathryn Scott. She happened to be in town when we recorded, and her presence on this song was the icing on the cake. Thanks, Kathryn.

So I'm asking you: How is your relationship with God right now? Not how was it five years ago or how do you hope it looks in days ahead; no, right now, in this moment, how is it? There's a good chance you may be just barely hanging on. You've had one of those days or one of those years when the hard stuff just kept coming and coming, and your cries for mercy seemed unheard. Please hang in there. Please hold on to the love of God. Don't let go. I can't tell you where He's taking you because I don't know.

But I can tell you that He is good. He is always good. He is our only hope.

God,
we hold on to so many
things for strength and comfort
and security and assurance.
But they're false, all of them.
Some of us know this from experience,
while the rest of us have yet to learn.
Please hold on to us.
Please don't let go.
You are our hope.
Amen.

CONTRIBUTING VOICES

My favorite line in this whole song is "I trust your heart, I trust your name." There is no safer place in the middle of life's stormy seas than the heart of God. There is no more radically honoring, protected hiding place for my heart than the place that is next to His.

I can trust His heart because He didn't send the storm. He's not behind it, but He is there in the very center of it with me. I can trust His heart because He is always, unswervingly, relentlessly good.

The video for this song has Paul singing in a theater in Colorado Springs as I sing on a harbor wall in Portstewart, Northern Ireland. It's really quite beautiful. As I stood there, singing "My Hope" out to Jesus while the waves crashed off that harbor wall, I was struck again by the strength of His kindness, the power of His goodness. I couldn't help but feel grounded by the safety of being able to trust His heart.

I'm beyond grateful for that solid ground under my feet. The truth is life is hard, but God is always good. That is the stuff of sustenance for the long haul, and the substance of hope that stands firm regardless of circumstance.

—Kathryn Scott

REIGN IN ME

With groanings too deep for words
I yearn for you, I yearn for you
With all of my weakness I come
In need of you, in need of you

Savior save me
Healer heal me
Jesus have your way
King of glory reign in me
Reign in me

I surrender to you alone
Your will be done, your will be done
With all of my heart I resign
My life to you, it's all for you

And forever I will say "you are good
And your promises will never fade away, never fade away"
You're pouring out your strength and your joy is everlasting
I will never be the same
I will never be the same

MARK 1:32–45

When dusk fell, the sick and haunted showed up at the door.
It seemed like everyone was outside. Jesus held the hands of
many of the sick and they were cured. For many chased by
darkness, He drove the evil away. The spirits knew who Jesus
was; He gave them clear instructions to keep quiet.

Later, in the dead of night, Jesus left the house and
found a lonely place to pray. Simon and others searched
till they finally found Him. *Everyone wants you.*

Jesus had a faraway look in His eyes. *The other towns nearby, they need to hear something good too. That's why I'm here.* So Jesus and His words visited the synagogues around Galilee, and He drove the darkness away.

A leper came and dropped to his knees before Jesus. *I'm begging you. Please take this away.*

His story broke Jesus's heart. Then Jesus did the unbelievable—He reached out and held the leper. *Now you're clean.* Just like that the man was made new.

Jesus was firm with Him. *Don't tell anyone. Go show yourself to the priest and make the required offering from Moses's law. That's all I want you to do.*

But that didn't happen. The man made new just had to tell somebody; in fact, he told everybody.

After that it was never the same for Jesus. He kept to the margins of the city, but even there the people found Him. They were coming from everywhere.

There's nothing I love more than singing with the saints, lifting holy hands with one another in the praise and adoration of our King. But sometimes there are moments after those intense worship experiences, moments when a strong feeling comes over me. I am immensely grateful for all of God's attributes and how they transform our lives, but sometimes, in those moments, I desperately need for God to be those things, well, for me.

I pray for God to rescue *us*,
but I also pray for God to rescue *me*.
I desire for God to put *us* on a path of
righteousness for His name's sake,
but I also desire Him to lead *me* beside
the still water and restore *my* soul.
Please, God, reign in *us*,
but please reign in *me*, too.

Now some people might hear that as an incredibly pathetic me-me-me attitude. But some people hear what they want to hear. I hear and experience it as a very humble approach, like the leper on his knees before Jesus, begging

Please take this away. His request was no doubt made in the presence of many pressing around Jesus, but it came solely from the bravery of the one. I've found we can be very childish in our approaches to God, and then we can be very childlike.

> When I was a child, I spake as a child,
> I understood as a child, I thought as a child:
> but when I became a man,
> I put away childish things.

> —1 Corinthians 13:11 (KJV)

So in a sense this song is a childlike prayer for grown-ups. Humility that says, "I need help, I cannot do this on my own." Humility that makes us crawl on our hands and knees out of desperation and hope that we will reach the One who can do for us what we cannot do for ourselves. Our personal pleas don't have to be some huge event with spotlights and music cues and the crowd's attention. No, God seems to be quite fond of men and women on their knees who bravely beg and plead.

Savior, save us,
and me.
Healer, heal us,
and me.
Jesus, have your way in us,
and in me.
King of glory, reign in us
as only You can reign.
But reign also in me.
I come as a child to You,
my Father,
our Father.
Amen.

LOOK UPON THE LORD

Look upon the Lord
Stand in awe of his beauty
Look upon the Lord
Seated high, He is holy

Let the glory of our God
From Heaven come down
Let the house of the Lord
Be filled with the cloud

You are good and your mercy will endure
You are good and forever we are yours
Hallelujah! Hallelujah!
Hallelujah! Hallelujah!

Listen for the Lord
Hear the voice of his spirit
Call upon his name
He is near, He is with us

Let the glory of our God
From Heaven come down
Let the house of the Lord
Be filled with the cloud

Holy, Holy, Holy
With one voice
Heaven and earth are singing

MARK 6:1–6

Then Jesus decided to go home, back to Nazareth, and His disciples followed. When the Sabbath rolled around, He made His way to the synagogue to teach and quickly gained an audience.

In one breath the crowd was off guard: *Is this Jesus? When did He get so smart?* But by the next breath they regained their composure: *A carpenter in the synagogue? C'mon, we know Him, this is Mary's son, brother to James, Joseph, Judas, and Simon, and those sisters.* However, His belonging unnerved them.

Jesus said, *You strain at the wonder before you because it looks familiar.*

They took Him for granted, so much so that Jesus's hands were tied; a handful of sick were healed, but that's all He could do. The hometown armor was impenetrable, their minds rolled up and closed long ago.

We were lingering after worship, trying to press further into God. The next thing I knew the glory of the Lord was filling the place, like something from the first three verses of 2 Chronicles 7.

> When Solomon finished praying, fire came down from heaven and consumed the burnt offering and the sacrifices, and the glory of the LORD filled the temple. The priests could not enter the temple of the LORD because the glory of the LORD filled it. When all the Israelites saw the fire coming down and the glory of the LORD above the temple, they knelt on the pavement with their faces to the ground, and they worshiped and gave thanks to the LORD, saying,
>
> "He is good; his love endures forever."
> (vv. 1–3 NIV)

I sensed the Holy Spirit clearly speaking as we were reminded of God's glory and goodness and love. It was one of those moments filled to the brim with wonder, this overwhelming sense of "wow" right there in the middle of a very familiar place and people. I was deeply convicted about the loss of wonder in our worship songs—no shame or guilt, but rather a sense of sadness concerning how good God is and how often we miss Him.

In the paraphrased scripture passage from Mark, the crowd's familiarity with Jesus became a barrier to His power. They thought they knew Him, who He was, where He came from, His strengths and weaknesses. But they missed His glory, the glory of the only begotten of God.

Wonder is tricky. You can't just snap your fingers and *voilà* it's there. No, it has to be stirred, and that was the goal with this song: to stir afresh our wonder of God. Wonder is anything taken for granted suddenly filled with mystery and awe and wow! Do we take God for granted sometimes? Sure. It's not this intentional thing, it just happens. It can happen to a marriage, a neighborhood, a friend, even a life. But when it does, the opportunities for God's power to be released are hindered. So being stirred to the wonder of God can also lead to being stirred to seeing and experiencing the *more* of our lives in Christ. That sounds wonderful, huh?

Lord,
forgive us for taking You
for granted.
We do not want familiarity
to hinder Your will and ways.
Stir afresh in us the
wonder of who You are,
Your glory and goodness
and love.
Holy, holy, holy
are You, Lord Almighty.
Amen.

KING OF HEAVEN

Jesus let your kingdom come here
Let your will be done here in us
Jesus there is no one greater
You alone are Savior
Show the world your love

King of heaven come down
King of heaven come now
Let your glory reign
Shining like the day
King of heaven come

King of heaven rise up
Who can stand against us
You are strong to save
In your mighty name
King of heaven come

We are children of your mercy
Rescued for your glory
We cry Jesus
Set our hearts towards you
That every eye would see you lifted high

King of Heaven come
King of Heaven come

MARK 4:33–41

Jesus kept telling stories that fit the moment. He was full of them. When it was just the Twelve He'd go back over everything, making sure they didn't lag behind.

When evening came He said, *I'd like to sail to the other side.* So the Twelve agreed and a few other boats came too.

A storm rose up out of nowhere, heaving waves large enough to swallow the boat. And where was Jesus? Asleep.

In confusion the disciples shook him. *Don't you care what happens to us?*

Jesus rose up and roared, *That is enough!*

The wind and waves knew His voice, and just like that the storm was over. He stared away but spoke to the disciples. *You must be fearless.*

The Twelve were terrified, asking one another, *What kind of man is this?*

We've been singing this song every Sunday at our church for the past year. It is easily one of my favorite songs on this project. It is an intercessory heart cry to the King of Heaven—*come down, Lord!* But it must be sung freely, dare I say boldly.

I grew up in the liturgical church, and one of the weekly aspects of the service is repeating the Lord's Prayer. The priest introduces that moment with something like, "As our Savior Christ has taught us, we are bold to say…" Wow, what an incredible line, to think that we are approaching the Master and Commander of the wind and the waves, the One who brought all creation into existence—the very King of Heaven—and we do not have to cower in fear before Him, but we can cry out with boldness for He has promised to hear our every prayer.

Did you catch the traces of the Lord's Prayer in the very beginning of the lyrics?

> *Let your kingdom come here*
> *Let your will be done here*

But both of those phrases end with the word *here*, as in "on earth." And that's what this cry is all about, asking the Lord to come down *here*—into our relationships that are fractured and hanging on by a thread; into our marriages that barely have a pulse; into our churches that seem to be straining at gnats and swallowing camels; into our own minds that wrestle with principalities and powers that pose as flesh and blood. We don't need some new age, diluted god who is powerless over creation. No, we're crying out to the Lord, the Ruler whose will is being done in heaven, and we want that same will to be done here, on earth, right now, not tomorrow, but today. King of Heaven, come down so that every eye will see and every heart will know that You are not like the other gods; You are the only One.

King of Heaven,
we are bold to say
Your kingdom come
Your will be done
here on earth,
in every aspect of our lives,

as it is being done in heaven.
Descend to us, we pray.
Amen.

CHRIST THE LORD

Son of God proved His love
That while we were sinners Jesus died for us
No more shame, no more fear
Our Savior is alive forever, God is near

Christ the Lord is risen today
The Lamb of God has taken our sins away
Love's redeeming work is done
Raise your voice! The King has overcome
Hallelujah, Hallelujah

By His grace, long ago
Our sins were as scarlet
Now they're white as snow
Love was nailed to the cross
His dying and his rising has changed our hearts

Made like Him, like Him we'll rise
Ours the cross, the grave, the sky

MARK 15:33–39

It was noon, but it might as well have been midnight. The darkness lasted a full three hours—thick, heavy, suffocating. At three o'clock Jesus cried out into the face of the darkness: *Eloi, Eloi, lama sabachthani?* His cry meant *My God, my God, why have you forgotten me?*

Some who remained heard Him and said, *It sounds like He's calling for Elijah.* Someone rushed to fill a sponge with wine and brought it back for Him to drink. *We'll see if Elijah comes to His rescue.*

With a final cry, Jesus's breath ran out. In that same breath the temple curtain split squarely down the center.

A Roman centurion was there beside the cross, taking it all in. He confessed, *There's no doubt in my mind. This man was the Son of God.*

I love the old hymn "Christ the Lord Is Risen Today." But I've always wondered why we sing it only once a year. I mean, I understand the Easter celebration connections, but we're Easter people, right? I've always believed we could sing that song every day. So that belief was behind this song, plus a little bit of "Okay, how can we make this song rock?"

I'm pleased with the result, not just because it does rock, but because we kept the integrity of the original song's theology intact, drawing from passages and verses like these:

> Therefore, since we have been justified through faith, we have peace with God

through our Lord Jesus Christ, through whom we have gained access by faith into this grace in which we now stand. And we boast in the hope of the glory of God. Not only so, but we also glory in our sufferings, because we know that suffering produces perseverance; perseverance, character; and character, hope. And hope does not put us to shame, because God's love has been poured out into our hearts through the Holy Spirit, who has been given to us.

You see, at just the right time, when we were still powerless, Christ died for the ungodly. Very rarely will anyone die for a righteous person, though for a good person someone might possibly dare to die. But God demonstrates his own love for us in this: While we were still sinners, Christ died for us.

—Romans 5:1–8 (NIV)

"Come now, let us settle the matter,"
    says the LORD.
"Though your sins are like scarlet,
    they shall be as white as snow;
though they are red as crimson,
    they shall be like wool."

—Isaiah 1:18 (NIV)

The chorus of the song is a declaration, this definitive statement of something accomplished, finished: *Love's redeeming work is done.* And that life-changing truth is followed by a call for us all to respond: *Raise your voice! Hallelujah! Hallelujah!*

My hope is this could be a year-round anthem for the redeemed to sing. We are Easter people, and we must proclaim this truth and respond with *hallelujahs* in every season of our lives. Christ is the Lord not just of one day, but of every day. Hallelujah!

Lamb of God,
there is no doubt in
our minds—
You are the Son of God.
May there be no doubt in
our voices too
as we raise them
in joyous praise to
Your mighty name!
Hallelujah! Hallelujah!
Amen.

CONCLUDING THOUGHTS

During the making of this album, my earthly father was passing away. My family and I tried spending as much time as possible that last year caring for him as his body was failing and he came closer to the end of his life. He'd had ninety-five healthy years and not until last year had anything seriously affected his well-being.

We all know that day will come, the day one or both of our parents pass away. Some of you already know the sense of loss that comes with losing a parent. I'd been preparing my heart, or so I thought, for the past twenty years, but that season has finally come. A season to let go. Besides the physical aspects of caring for him this past year, what I've noticed is how strong the desire is to honor him—to express thanks to him for so many things he has done for us, his children. I found myself wanting to give thanks and affirm the qualities about him that we have noticed and admired for years, but perhaps didn't speak out loud.

As a family we spent time with my dad, looking at pictures of his life from the time he was born until some of his most recent events. We've been watching old home movies from the past several decades that chronicle the seasons of his life and tell the story of a man who faithfully cared for his widowed mother and supported his younger sister who was afflicted with polio until a week before his wedding to my mom in his early thirties. There are pictures and movies of him diving, dancing, golfing, having catches with the kids, working on the cars, and so on. I am so grateful for these reminders of his life.

Forgive the obvious analogy, but it sounds similar to the condition of the heart and the expressions we often use in our worship of God—our heavenly Father. We dwell on who God is, His character, His attributes, His deeds, and this is the foundation that our worship is based on. Again, I'm struck with the parallels. The only way we get to know the God we worship is to study Him, meditate on Him, and reflect on Him. This occurs through His creation, and our experiences, but most of all—through His Word.

My prayer is that the songs on *The Same Love* and the devotional thoughts from this book will help you remember who God is and what He has done. May you be inspired to live a life that expresses gratitude and honor to your Father in heaven.

SONG CREDITS

"The Same Love" by Paul Baloche & Michael Rossback © 2012 Integrity Worship Music/LeadWorship Songs (all adm at www.EMICMGPublishing.com).

"We Are Saved" by Paul Baloche, Ben Fielding, & Jason Ingram © 2012 Integrity Worship Music/LeadWorship Songs (adm at www.EMICMGPublishing.com) & Sony/ATV Music Publishing LLC/West Main Music/Windsor Music & Ben Fielding/Hillsong Publishing.

"King of Heaven" by Paul Baloche & Jason Ingram © 2012 Integrity Worship Music/LeadWorship Songs (adm at www.EMICMGPublishing.com) & Sony/ATV Music Publishing LLC/West Main Music/Windsor Music.

"All Because of the Cross" by Paul Baloche & Ben Gowell *Contains portions of "Nothing but the Blood" by Robert Lowry.* New words and music and this arr. © 2012